Parent's Introduction

Whether your child is a beginning reader, a reluctant reader, or an eager reader, this book offers a fun and easy way to encourage and help your child in reading.

Developed with reading education specialists, **We Both Read** books invite you and your child to take turns reading aloud. You read the left-hand pages of the book, and your child reads the right-hand pages—which have been written at one of six early reading levels. The result is a wonderful new reading experience and faster reading development!

You may find it helpful to read the entire book aloud your-self the first time, then invite your child to participate the second time. As you read, try to make the story come alive by reading with expression. This will help to model good fluency. It will also be helpful to stop at various points to discuss what you are reading. This will help increase your child's understanding of what is being read.

In some books, a few challenging words are introduced in the parent's text, distinguished with **bold** lettering. Pointing out and discussing these words can help to build your child's reading vocabulary. If your child is a beginning reader, it may be helpful to run a finger under the text as each of you reads. Please also notice that a "talking parent" ⊙ icon precedes the parent's text, and a "talking child" ⊙ icon precedes the child's text.

If your child struggles with a word, you can encourage "sounding it out," but keep in mind that not all words can be sounded out. Your child might pick up clues about a word from the picture, other words in the sentence, or any rhyming patterns. If your child struggles with a word for more than five seconds, it is usually best to simply say the word.

Most of all, remember to praise your child's efforts and keep the reading fun. After you have finished the book, ask a few questions and discuss what you have read together. Rereading this book multiple times may also be helpful for your child.

Try to keep the tips above in mind as you read together, but don't worry about doing everything right. Simply sharing the enjoyment of reading together will increase your child's reading skills and help to start your child off on a lifetime of reading enjoyment!

A Day on the International Space Station

A We Both Read® Book
Level 2

With special thanks to personnel in the Public Affairs Department at NASA
for their review and recommendations on the material in this book

Images provided by NASA.
Text Copyright © 2018 by Larry Swerdlove
All rights reserved

We Both Read® is a registered trademark of Treasure Bay, Inc.

Published by
Treasure Bay, Inc.
P. O. Box 119
Novato, CA 94948 USA

Printed in Malaysia

Library of Congress Control Number: 2017937641

Paperback ISBN: 978-1-60115-302-9

Visit us online at:
TreasureBayBooks.com

PR-11-17

WE BOTH READ®

A DAY ON THE INTERNATIONAL
SPACE STATION

by Larry Swerdlove

TREASURE BAY

👓 Good Morning, Earth

Here on Earth we usually sleep at night and get out of bed when the sun comes up in the morning. However, an **astronaut** on the International Space Station doesn't sleep only at night, and the sun doesn't come up only once a day. When you are orbiting high above Earth, traveling over 17,000 miles an hour, the sun rises every 90 minutes!

Astronauts float
even while sleeping.

Straps hold their
sleeping bags in place.

Astronauts go to
sleep in their own little
bedrooms. When they
live in space, this is
their home away from
home. These astronauts
have a busy day. It's
time to get out of bed!

☉ What Is the International Space Station?

The International Space Station is a large spacecraft that orbits **Earth**. For many years, astronauts have lived and worked there. Many countries worked together to build this giant science laboratory. Including the solar panels, the **space station** is the size of a football field. It flies about 250 miles above Earth. That's over 30 times higher than most airplanes fly!

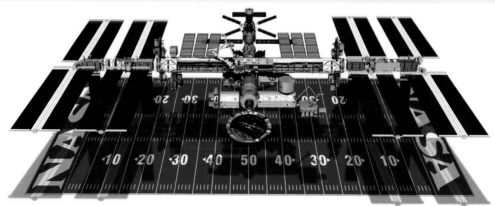

Size of space station compared to a football field

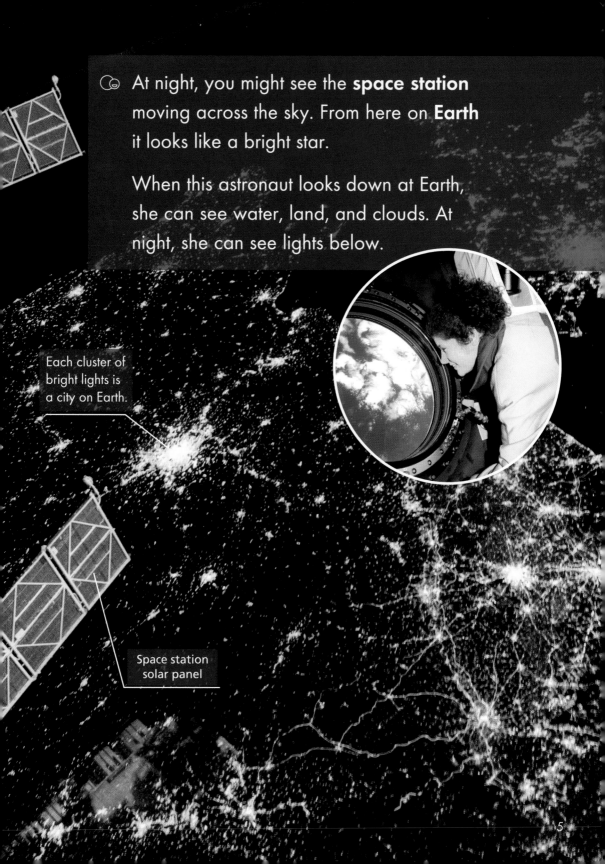

At night, you might see the **space station** moving across the sky. From here on **Earth** it looks like a bright star.

When this astronaut looks down at Earth, she can see water, land, and clouds. At night, she can see lights below.

Each cluster of bright lights is a city on Earth.

Space station solar panel

This is an **illustration** for a space station that was never built.

Rocket launch for Skylab in 1973

Salyut 7

⊛ Earlier Space Stations

Even before humans went into space, scientists started designing a "space platform" where astronauts could live and work. An early design looked like a big wheel, but it was never actually built.

Russia built the first space station. It was called Salyut (SAL-yoot). It was launched in 1971. In 1973, the **United States** created **Skylab**, which stayed in orbit for six years.

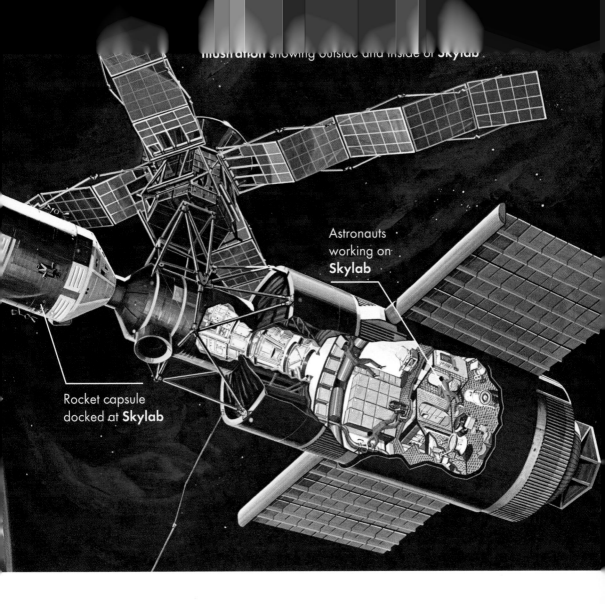

Astronauts
working on
Skylab

Rocket capsule
docked at **Skylab**

Then the **United States** and **Russia** teamed up with others to build a new space station. They wanted to make the biggest and best space station ever built.

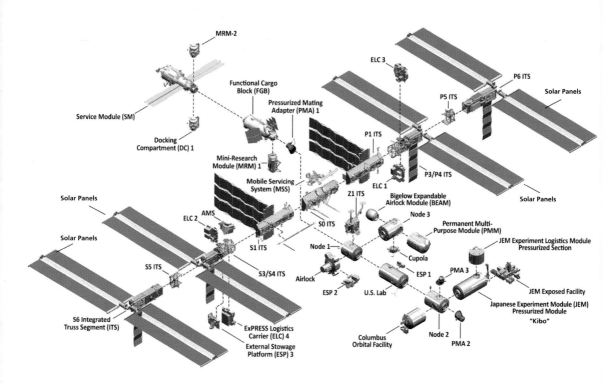

The pieces of the International Space Station
have been put together in space.

⊙ Modules and Nodes on the International Space Station

The International Space Station is made up of **modules** and **nodes**. **Modules** are like rooms. **Nodes** connect the larger modules together. It is all put together like a giant toy construction set.

Each piece has many openings, called *hatches*, which can connect to the other pieces. There are **modules** that are living spaces, storage units, research labs, and equipment modules.

Space Shuttle docked at the space station during early construction

A **module** is about the size of a school bus. **Nodes** are much smaller. Besides modules and nodes, there are also docks. A dock is where visiting astronauts park their spaceships.

Launch of the Space Shuttle

Unity node is prepared for its launch to the space station.

⚭ How the Space Station Was Built

The space station started small. The first module was called **Zarya** (zer-YAW). It was launched by Russian **scientists** in 1998, but **Zarya** didn't have the air and water systems needed by astronauts to live in space.

A few weeks later, the United States sent the Space Shuttle *Endeavour* to deliver the second piece of the space station. It was a node called Unity, which was designed with six ports, so it could connect up to six modules together.

Unity node

Over time, **scientists** sent up more parts of the space station. The pieces were put together in space. They had to fit together perfectly.

Zarya module

A special airplane and flight pattern lets astronauts experience short periods of floating in air.

Training for launch into space

Training for Space

Today there are over 500 astronauts in the world. They come from many places including the United States, Russia, Europe, and Japan.

In the United States, future astronauts are selected and trained by NASA. The training program takes about two years to complete. During the program, astronauts spend a lot of time learning about things like navigation, astronomy, physics, computers, weather, and safety. They also have to learn how to put on a space suit, which they need to wear if they go outside the space station.

How long does it take you to get dressed? Getting into a space suit is tricky. This astronaut is learning how to put on his space suit. It takes him about 20 minutes to put everything on.

Space suits weigh about 300 pounds!

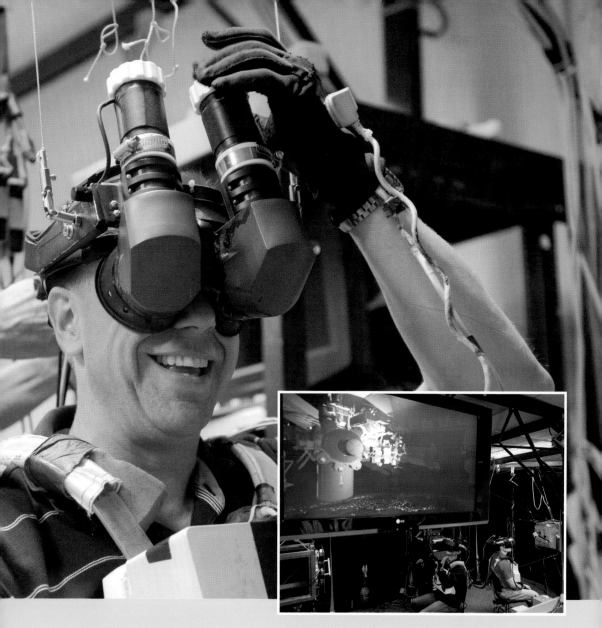

Do you like playing video games? Well, these astronauts spend many hours practicing on simulators, which are like very fancy video games. In order to **practice** what it is like to work in space, astronauts spend weeks in the Virtual Reality Lab in Houston, Texas, which has the coolest "games" on Earth! Each "game" lasts three to eight hours.

This astronaut is practicing what he may have to do during a spacewalk outside the space station.

To **practice** floating in space, astronauts use a huge swimming pool. There are full-size models of space station parts in the water. Astronauts can practice fixing things while floating.

Crew capsule about to dock at the space station

Now the capsule is docked and locked in place.

Another capsule is docked here.

⊚ Getting to the International Space Station

Every few months, new astronauts are flown up to the International Space Station. It takes about six hours to reach the space station from Earth. Trying to dock the capsule with the space station is not easy when you're traveling over 17,000 miles per hour. Each astronaut will spend months at a time living and working in space.

When the capsule comes back to Earth, a parachute helps to slow its descent.

A capsule has landed in the middle of a farm.

It may take six hours to get to the space station, but it only takes a little more than three hours to return home. That's faster than it takes to fly across the United States in a plane.

Astronauts float around the space station.

◎◎ Weightlessness

There are no ceilings or floors on the International Space Station. That's because there is no up or down in space.

There isn't any normal **gravity** to hold a person down, so astronauts don't have to walk-instead, they can fly! Without **gravity**, astronauts can pick up things that weigh hundreds of pounds on Earth. And they can do it with just one hand!

It's hard for this astronaut to keep her hair neat. She could try brushing it, but without **gravity** it will not stay down. It will just fly around. Gravity is what keeps everything from floating around on Earth.

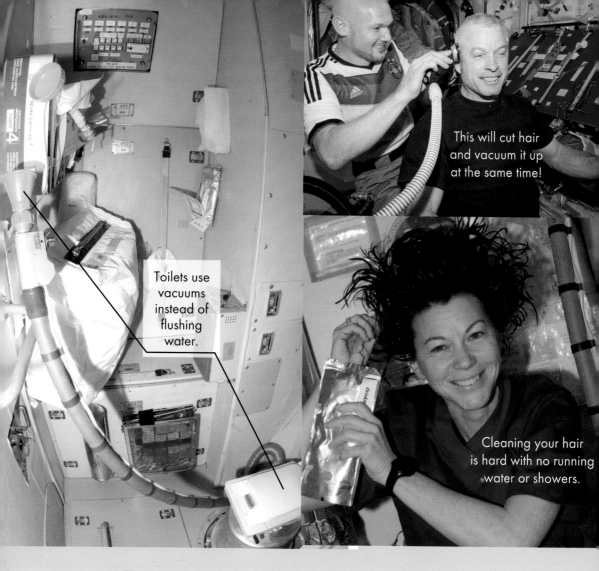

This will cut hair and vacuum it up at the same time!

Toilets use vacuums instead of flushing water.

Cleaning your hair is hard with no running water or showers.

👓 The Bathroom

Cleaning up in the morning can be a challenge in space. Astronauts are given a kit with everything they need, including a toothbrush, **toothpaste**, and a hair brush.

There are no faucets with running water because the water wouldn't flow down. It would just float around. So washing is done with a soapy towel.

You can't spit out the toothpaste!

Without a sink, these astronauts have to swallow their **toothpaste** or spit it into a towel when they are finished brushing. All of their things have to be strapped down so they don't float away.

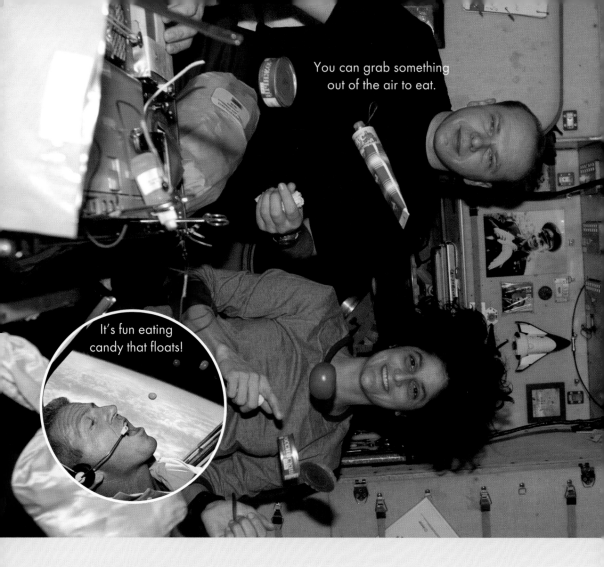

You can grab something out of the air to eat.

It's fun eating candy that floats!

🔗 The Galley

It's breakfast time! Food is served in the galley-an open area where the crew shares meals together. Most of the food is stored in little pouches and doesn't need much preparation.

Coffee and juice are also served in pouches because liquids float around the room in bubbles. Sometimes it's hard to resist playing with your food when it's floating around you.

Drinks come in pouches.

Meals float, so you can't use a plate.

Astronauts are allowed to bring some of their favorite foods from Earth. Some bring noodles. Others bring cookies. One astronaut even brought a jar of peanut butter. What kind of food would you bring to the space station?

This is what the Cupola looks like from outside the space station.

⚭ The Cupola

The Cupola (KYOO-puh-luh) is a small room with a lot of windows. It's a favorite place for astronauts to relax when they aren't doing experiments or fixing things. From the Cupola astronauts can watch the weather on Earth change from day to day.

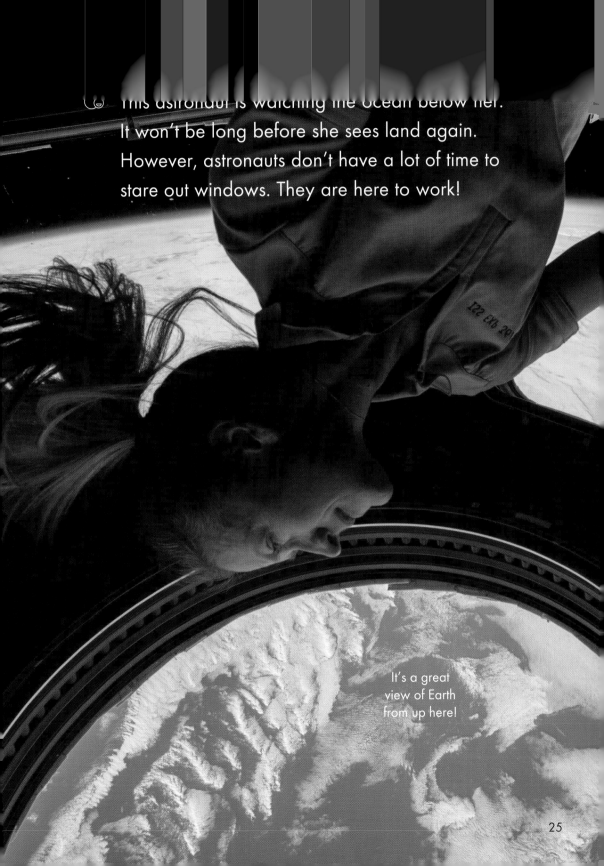

This astronaut is watching the ocean below her. It won't be long before she sees land again. However, astronauts don't have a lot of time to stare out windows. They are here to work!

It's a great view of Earth from up here!

There are a lot of machines and experiments to work on.

"Check this out!"

How do plants grow in space?

Research on the International Space Station

These astronauts are conducting **experiments** in the biggest module on the station. The **Kibo** (KIH-boh) module was built in Japan as a scientific laboratory.

Scientists from all over the world send **experiments** to the space station to test their ideas and learn how life is different in space. Some study plants. Others study how the weather works. Some even study how ants behave without gravity.

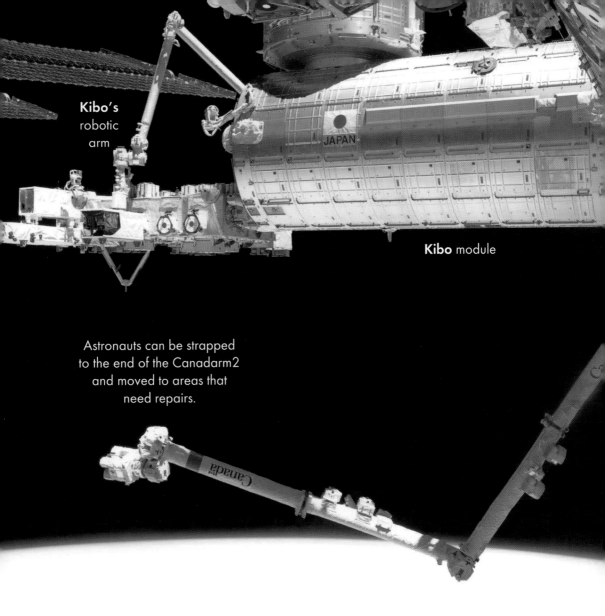

Kibo's robotic arm

JAPAN

Kibo module

Astronauts can be strapped to the end of the Canadarm2 and moved to areas that need repairs.

Canada

◠◡ **Kibo** is the biggest module on the space station. Many **experiments** are done inside and outside this module.

Kibo has a 32-foot-long robotic arm that is used for working outside the station. Another robotic arm, called the Canadarm2, is 57 feet long.

Golden orb spider

⊙ Experiments in the Space Station

These astronauts are learning how spiders jump in space. The idea came from a teenager in Egypt. Many school children send their ideas to the scientists on the space station. Do you have an idea for a space experiment?

Someday humans will travel to places far from Earth. To see how space affects the human body, a lot of experiments are done on the astronauts themselves.

Do you think it is easier or harder to work while floating?

Learning how to live in space for a long time is important. Because there is no gravity in space, astronauts don't use their muscles very much. This can make them very weak.

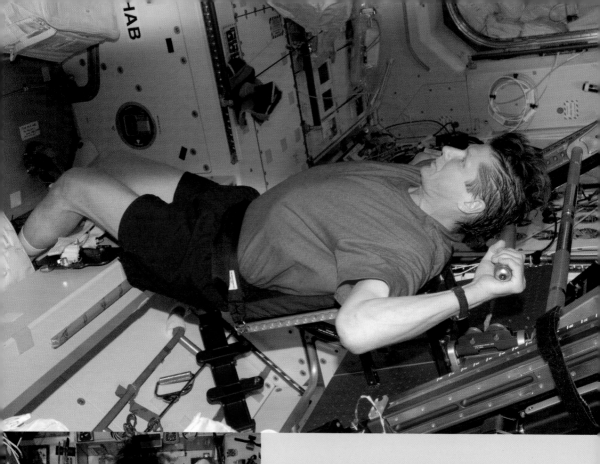

When you run on a treadmill, you have to be strapped into place!

⚭ Exercise Is Important

To fight against bone and muscle loss, every astronaut has to exercise about two hours a day. Although they are inside the spacecraft, they can ride a **stationary** bike, run on a treadmill, or even pump some iron. Scientists have developed equipment that can work in weightlessness. Some of the equipment requires seat belts.

 On the space station there is no up or down, no ceilings or floors. So in this photo, it only looks like this astronaut is riding a **stationary** bide upside down.

This astronaut can use his jetpack to get back to the space station.

☺ Spacewalks

Spacewalks are done in order to install new equipment, make repairs, and do experiments on the outside of the space station. Astronauts need space suits to keep them safe and comfortable when they are not inside the spacecraft. The huge backpack provides power, oxygen, and water. There is also a jetpack in case they get separated from the space station.

Outside the space station there is no air. If the sun is out, it is very, very hot. When it gets dark, it is very, very cold. Space suits protect the astronauts and keep them safe during spacewalks.

You can see a lot of land and oceans from the space station.

For safety, astronauts stay connected to the space station.

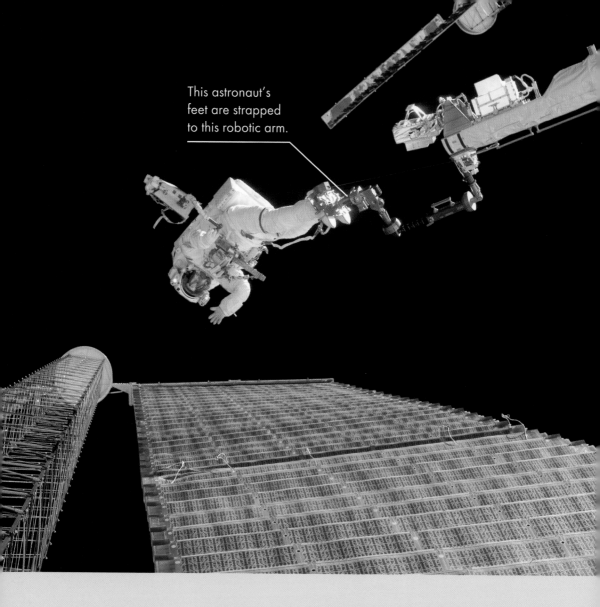

This astronaut's feet are strapped to this robotic arm.

Today's job is to repair one of the solar panels. The panels hold more than 250,000 solar cells. They supply all the power for the International Space Station and must be pointed toward the sun at all times.

Astronauts strap their feet onto the long robotic arm in order to reach the part of the space station that needs work.

Entrance to an airlock to get back into the space station

Astronaut coming out of the airlock

👀 Very soon the sun will set again. When the sun is hidden behind Earth, it gets very cold and dark outside the space station.

Now that the repair is done, it's time to go back inside.

⊕ The Robonaut

It can be dangerous working outside of the space station. The temperatures are extreme and there's lots of radiation. There is even space junk flying around that could harm an astronaut.

To make working in space safer, NASA and General Motors developed the **Robonaut**, a life-size humanoid robot. The **Robonaut** can be controlled by astronauts like a remote-controlled puppet.

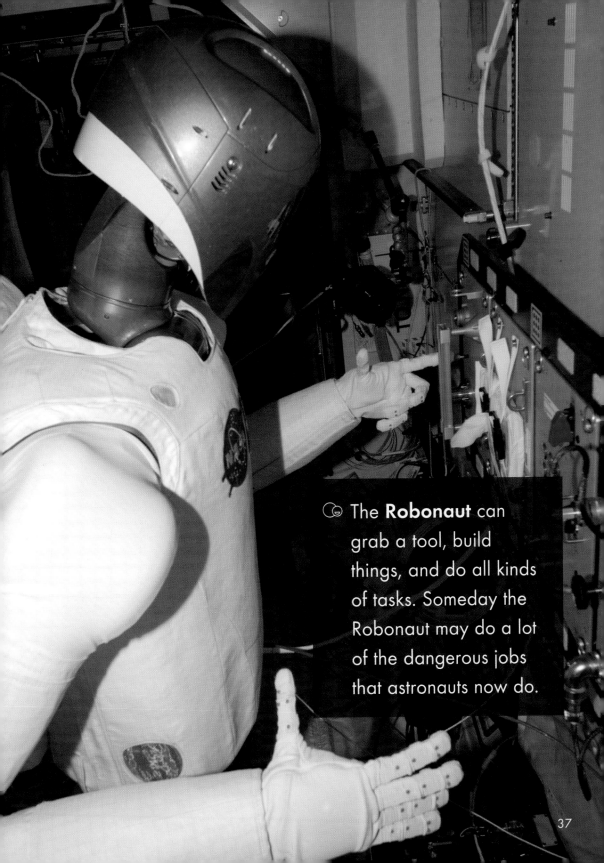

The **Robonaut** can grab a tool, build things, and do all kinds of tasks. Someday the Robonaut may do a lot of the dangerous jobs that astronauts now do.

These astronauts aren't really upside down. They're just floating in the space station!

Astronauts Wanted

An astronaut's job is very important. Every day, Mission Control plans each astronaut's work schedule. The work that is done in space will help people on Earth prepare for the future. Experiments done on the International Space Station will lead to new discoveries that will help in medical treatments, protecting Earth's environment, and future space travel.

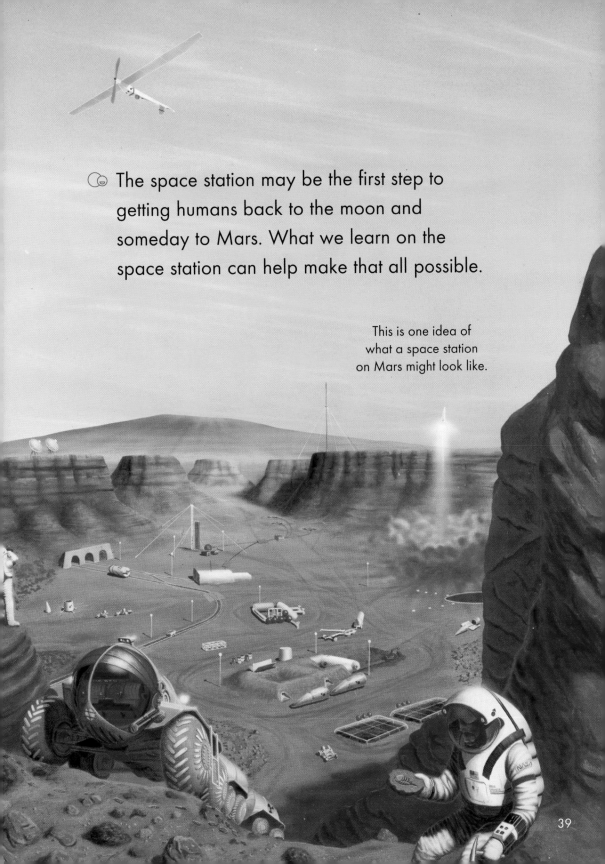

The space station may be the first step to getting humans back to the moon and someday to Mars. What we learn on the space station can help make that all possible.

This is one idea of what a space station on Mars might look like.

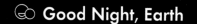 Good Night, Earth

All **people** need to sleep, and at the end of the day the astronauts return to their sleep stations. They have to strap themselves in so they don't float away while they sleep. This astronaut has already seen 11 sunrises today, and there will be 5 more while he sleeps. **Imagine** that!

All kinds of **people** become astronauts: doctors, teachers, pilots, people who like math and science, and others. They are people who like adventure and want to do something important. Maybe someday you could become an astronaut. **Imagine** that!

If you would like to learn more about the International Space Station or see what's new, you can talk with your parents or teachers about going to these websites:

http://www.nasa.gov/mission_pages/station/research/ops/research_student.html

http://iss.jaxa.jp/kids/en/

http://www.sciencekids.co.nz/sciencefacts/space/internationalspacestation.html

http://www.esa.int/esaKIDSen/

The web address below is for a page on the NASA website that has video tours of the space station:

https://www.nasa.gov/mission_pages/station/main/suni_iss_tour.html

The web addresses above were active at the time of publication. We apologize if any of them are no longer active.

If you liked **A Day on the International Space Station,** here are some other We Both Read® books you are sure to enjoy!

To see all the We Both Read books that are available, just go online to **www.WeBothRead.com**.